Aesop's Fables

Retold by
Carol Watson

Adapted by Katie Daynes

Illustrated by
Nick Price

Reading Consultant: Alison Kelly
Roehampton University

Contents

Introduction

The mystery writer

These stories were first told so long ago, no one knows who really wrote them. They may have been written by a man called Aesop*, who lived in Greece thousands of years ago.

* say ee-sop

No one knows much about Aesop either. He might have been a slave... or a king. But everyone agrees the stories are great. And they all have one thing in common.

What does this tell you?

Every story is a fable. This means it has a moral, or a lesson to be learned. See if you can guess the moral before the story ends.

4

Chapter 1

The tortoise and the hare

One day, the hare was boasting about how amazingly fast he could run. His friends just yawned. They'd heard it all before.

The hare started to pick on the old tortoise.

"You're so slow, I'm surprised you ever get anywhere," he teased.

A snail could run faster than you!

"I may be slow," replied the tortoise, "but I bet I can reach the end of this field before you."

"Hooray, a challenge!" whooped the hare. "Come on everyone. Watch me win!"

The other animals gathered around as the hare and the tortoise lined up to start.

"Ready, steady, go!" shouted the
badger. Everyone cheered as
the hare raced off, leaving
the tortoise
far behind.

The tortoise wasn't bothered. She
plodded along at
her own speed.

What's
the rush?

Halfway across the field, the hare looked back over his shoulder.

"That old tortoise will take all day," he thought. "I might as well have a little rest."

Zzzzzzz...

Soon he had fallen fast asleep in the warm sunshine.

Several hours later, the hare woke up in a panic. In the distance, he could see the tortoise about to cross the finishing line. He ran as fast as he could, but it was too late. The tortoise had won.

Who's the slow one now?

And the moral is...
Slow but sure can win the race.

Chapter 2

The thirsty crow

One hot summer, a thirsty crow
was searching for something to
drink. It hadn't rained for weeks
and he was beginning to give
up hope.

Then in the distance he spied a
pot on someone's windowsill.
He flew over
to take a
closer look.

Please let
there be some
water inside.

He could see water, but he couldn't

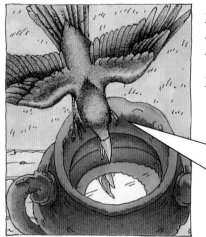

reach it. Now
he felt even
more thirsty.

How will I ever
drink that?

"Maybe I could break the pot..."
he thought.
But his
beak wouldn't
crack the
hard clay.

"If I could just knock the
pot over..."
He pushed
with all his
weight but
the pot
wouldn't
budge.

The crow felt very sorry for himself... until he had an idea. He flew to a pile of pebbles, picked them up one by one and dropped them into the pot.

Each pebble pushed the water up a little higher, until the crow could finally take a sip.

The cold water tasted wonderful and the crow congratulated himself on being so clever.

And the moral is...
Try hard enough and you'll get what you want.

Chapter 3

The ant and the dove

On his way home, an ant saw a
sparkling fountain. He crawled
onto its wall to take a closer look.

The next thing he knew, he had slipped into the water. He gurgled and panicked and waved his legs in the air.

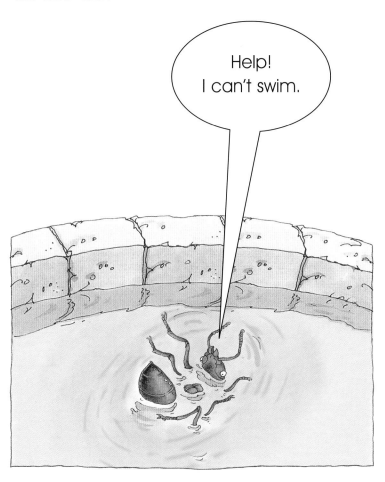

Luckily, just at that moment, a friendly dove flew by. She saw that the tiny ant was drowning and quickly flew to a nearby tree.

She pulled off a leaf and let it
glide down to the ant.

"Here you are," she cooed,
and flew away.

The ant struggled onto the leaf. He breathed a sigh of relief as he floated to safety.

The following day, he saw his rescuer in a field. The dove was out looking for worms... and she wasn't alone.

The ant knew the dove was in trouble, but what could he do?

With one swoop of his net, the man trapped the dove. "You're coming with me, my beauty," he cried.

"Not if I can help it," thought the ant. He ran up the man's leg and bit him.

Ouch!

The man yelped and dropped the net to clutch his leg.

"Thank you my little friend," cooed the dove, as she flew away.

And the moral is...
One good turn deserves another.

Chapter 4

The fox and the stork

One evening, a sly fox invited a
hungry stork to dinner.

"Make yourself at home while I
serve our meal," said the fox.

24

The stork sat down. Delicious spicy smells wafted in from the kitchen.

"Here we are," said the fox, carrying two steaming bowls of fresh soup.

This should be amusing.

The fox greedily lapped up his soup and eyed the stork's bowl. The stork was having trouble. Her beak was too long to eat from the fox's shallow dish.

Let me help you finish it off.

She flew home in a bad mood, feeling very hungry.

"That cunning fox tricked me and ate my dinner too," she squawked, and plotted how to get back at him.

A week later, the stork invited the fox to dinner.

"Your soup was so delicious," she said, "I thought I'd make some too."

The stork poured the soup into two tall jars. She ate hers easily, but the fox hadn't a chance. His nose was far too short.

"I've been fooled by my own trick," he sighed.

And the moral is...
Play mean tricks on people and they may play them back on you.

Chapter 5

The mouse's tale

A little brown mouse lived happily
under a hedge in the countryside.

30

One day his cousin from town
came to visit.

"I thought I'd try out life in the
country," he said.

You'll love
it here!

The country mouse did
everything he could to look after
his city cousin. He gave him the
best piece of moss to sleep on
and fed him his tastiest nuts
and vegetables.

The town mouse wasn't impressed. He found the food horrible and the life boring.

"Why don't we both go back to the town?" he suggested.

We can have some real fun.

So off they went. On the way, the town mouse told his cousin how they would dine like kings.

As night fell, they arrived at
a large town house.

"This way," whispered the town
mouse, scrambling under the
back door.

Up a flight of stairs and down a long hall they found the dining room... and the dining room table.

The country mouse couldn't believe his eyes.

"I've never seen this much food!" he squeaked.

They were nibbling away
when the door opened and in
came a man.

The two cousins hid and held
their breath. The
man came closer,
peered in the
fruit bowl,
took an apple
and left.

"All clear," said the town mouse.
But his little cousin was too scared

to eat any
more.

Swiss cheese
is so tasty!

In the corner, a large cat was woken up by all the noise. He padded across to the table and spotted the two mice.

The country mouse squealed as
the cat sprang onto the table.
"Follow me!" cried his cousin and
they dived into a mouse hole.

The country mouse was
very frightened.

"This isn't my idea of fun," he
sniffed. "I'm sorry cousin, but
I'm going back to the peaceful
countryside."

Come back and visit soon.

He waved the town mouse
goodbye and set off for his comfy
little home under a hedge.

And the moral is...
*A simple, quiet life beats a rich,
dangerous one.*

Chapter 6

The dog and the bone

One day, a naughty dog stole a
big, juicy bone from the butcher.

The dog scampered away across the fields...

...and onto a bridge that crossed a stream.

He looked down at the water and jumped in surprise. There was another dog staring up at him and he had a big, juicy bone in his mouth too.

His bone's bigger than mine...

He growled at the dog and the dog growled back.

"I want *your* bone," barked the dog on the bridge.

Give it to me!

But, as he opened his mouth, his bone slipped out.

It fell into the water with a
big splash.

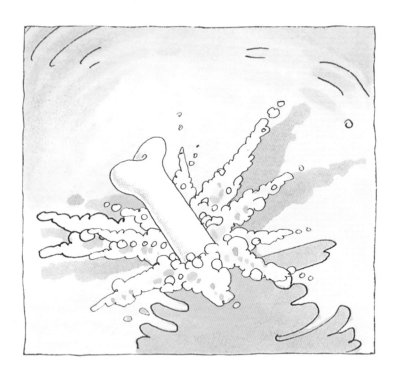

When the ripples cleared, all the
dog could see was himself. There
had never been another dog, and
now there was no bone either.

And the moral is...
Be happy with what you have.

Chapter 7

The fox and the crow

A fox was out for a stroll when he saw a crow perched up in a tree.

The crow had stolen a lump of cheese. She was feeling very pleased with herself.

"I'd like that cheese for myself," thought the fox.

He stopped under the tree and started to tell the crow how lovely she looked.

Wow! I've never seen a bird as stunning as you. You have such pretty feathers...

The crow
believed
every word.

"I suppose
I am quite
beautiful,"
she thought.

"I bet
you have an
amazing
voice as well,"
continued
the fox.

"I do!" thought the crow, wanting to show off her voice. She opened her beak and gave a loud "caw". Out dropped the cheese, straight into the fox's mouth.

Yum!

And the moral is...
Don't be fooled by flattery.

Chapter 8

The lion and the mouse

Zzzzzzz...

It was too hot to prowl, so the king of the jungle lay snoozing in the sun.

A tiny mouse was hurrying home with some corn for her dinner. She was in such a rush, she didn't notice the lion and ran straight over his paw.

The lion felt
a tickle and
woke up.

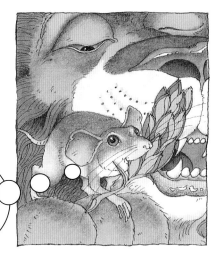

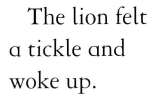

He grabbed the mouse in his

claws.
    "A mouse
for dinner,
what a nice
idea," he
snarled and
licked his lips.

"Please don't eat me," squeaked
the mouse. "Let me go and I
promise I'll help you out one day."

"Ha! You really think a little
mouse like you can help a lion like
me," he sneered.

But he admired the mouse's
bravery, so he let her go.

The next day, the lion was out hunting when he tripped on a rope and set off a trap. A large net fell on him.

He struggled to free himself, but the net held him tightly.

"How dare someone trap the king of the jungle," he cried, and his voice echoed through the trees.

Far away, the mouse heard the lion's roar.

"I promised to help him and so I shall," she thought.

She ran through the jungle as fast as she could.

"I'm here to rescue you," she told the lion.

"Fat chance," he replied, but there was no one else to help.

The mouse nibbled and gnawed at the net until at last the lion was free.

"I was wrong to doubt you, little mouse," he said. "Thank you for saving my life."

Goodbye, my friend.

And the moral is...
Little friends can be great friends.

If you enjoyed these stories, there are lots more you can read!

Try these other books in
Series Two:

Hercules: Hercules was the world's first superhero. But even superheroes have a hard time when faced with twelve impossible tasks.

King Arthur: Arthur is just a boy, until he pulls a sword out of a stone. Suddenly, he is King of England. The trouble is, not everyone wants him on the throne.

The Fairground Ghost: When Jake goes to the fair he wants a really scary ride. But first, he must teach the fairground ghost a trick or two.

The Amazing Adventures of Ulysses: Ulysses tries to rescue a princess and gets caught up in a ten-year war. Here, you can follow the story of his incredible voyage home.

Additional Illustrations: Ian McNee

Series editor: Lesley Sims

Designed by
Katarina Dragoslavić

This edition first published in 2007 by Usborne Publishing Ltd.,
Usborne House, 83-85 Saffron Hill, London EC1N 8RT, England.
www.usborne.com
Copyright © 2007, 2003, 1982 Usborne Publishing Ltd.